JBIOG
Seuss
Adil, Janeen R.

Dr. Seuss : great story
teller /

Dr. Seuss

GREAT STORY TELLER

by
Janeen R. Adil

P.O. Box 196
Hockessin, Delaware 19707
Visit us on the web: www.mitchelllane.com
Comments? email us: mitchelllane@mitchelllane.com

Mitchell Lane
PUBLISHERS

Printing   1   2   3   4   5   6   7   8

A Robbie Reader

Hillary Duff	Thomas Edison	Albert Einstein
Philo T. Farnsworth	Henry Ford	Robert Goddard
Mia Hamm	Tony Hawk	LeBron James
Donovan McNabb	**Dr. Seuss**	Charles Schulz

Library of Congress Cataloging-in-Publication Data
Adil, Janeen R.-
     Dr. Seuss / by Janeen R. Adil.
          p. cm. — (A Robbie reader)
    Includes bibliographical references (p.) and index.
     ISBN 1-58415-288-5 (library bound)
    1. Seuss, Dr. — Juvenile literature. 2. Authors, American--20th century — Biography — Juvenile literature. 3. Illustrators — United States — Biography — Juvenile literature. 4. Children's literature — Authorship — Juvenile literature. I. Title. II. Series.
PS3513.E2Z54 2004
813'.52--dc22
                                        2004009301

ABOUT THE AUTHOR: A former teacher, Janeen R. Adil writes for children and adults. Her work includes books, magazine and Web site articles, and more. Although she's written on a wide range of topics, her favorites are nature subjects, history, and biographies. In 2003 she was awarded the Trudy Farrand and John Strohm Magazine Writing Award by *Ranger Rick* magazine of the National Wildlife Federation. A New England native, Janeen now lives with her family in eastern Pennsylvania.

PHOTO CREDITS: Cover: Getty Images; pp. 4, 6, 8, 10, 12, 14 Getty Images; p. 16 Hulton/Archive; p. 18 Nancy Palmieri/AP Photo; p. 20 Roswell Daily Record; p. 22 Vince Bucci/Stringer; p. 23 Hulton/Archive; p. 26 Kim Johnson/AP Photo; p. 28 Vince Bucci/Stringer.

ACKNOWLEDGMENTS: The following story has been thoroughly researched, and to the best of our knowledge, represents a true story. While every possible effort has been made to ensure accuracy, the publisher will not assume liability for damages caused by inaccuracies in the data, and makes no warranty on the accuracy of the information contained herein. This story has not been authorized nor endorsed by anyone associated with Dr. Seuss' estate.

TABLE OF CONTENTS

Dr. Seuss was really Theodor Seuss Geisel. He used Dr. Seuss as a "pen name."

A POUNDING BEAT

All day long the ship's engines made the same sound. *Da da DUM, da da DUM, da da DUM, da da DUM.* Over and over they pounded out this beat. Ted Geisel (GUY-zil) couldn't get the sound out of his head.

The year was 1936. Ted and his wife, Helen, were sailing from the United States to Europe. On the ship, Ted started making notes for a children's story. The same words kept going through his head. "And that is a story that no one can beat" was stuck in his mind. He had written this line to the beat of the ship's engines.

During his life, Ted wrote 44 books for children.

When he got home, Ted kept on writing. Each line of the story had that same beat. He drew fantastic pictures for his story, too. *And to Think That I Saw It on Mulberry Street* was Ted's first children's book. He published it in 1937.

Ted wrote more and more books for children. He wrote 44 children's books over his lifetime. But Ted didn't sign his name to these books. He used a different name, Dr. Seuss. Not many people knew that Dr. Seuss was really Ted Geisel. Dr. Seuss is what is called a "pen name."

Pages from *Fox in Sox,* published in 1965.

Ted liked children but could be shy with grown-ups.

BIG IDEAS

Theodor Seuss Geisel was born on March 2, 1904, in Springfield, Massachusetts. His father, Theodor Robert Geisel, taught him the value of working hard. His mother, Henrietta Seuss Geisel, helped him think up new ideas. Ted loved to dream up pictures and words. He played with different ideas, like drawing a tiger with wings.

Ted had two sisters. Henrietta died when she was very little. Marnie was his older sister. Marnie and Ted were friends all their lives.

Ted's family was German. He was very proud of that fact. The Geisels spoke German at home. They had fun times with other German families in town.

Ted worked very hard on each book. He wanted to make the words and pictures just right.

Living in Springfield gave Ted ideas for his books. His town had big parades, like the one in *Mulberry Street.* And for a while, his father ran the zoo. Ted spent hours there, drawing the animals. Later, he made the book *If I Ran the Zoo.*

Ted went to Central High School. He took an art class but stayed for only one day. His teacher said that art had rules to follow. Ted had his own ideas, though. "I wanted to draw things as I saw them," he said.

Ted was happier working on the school paper. He wrote, made up jokes, and drew cartoons. When he went to college, Ted drew more cartoons. His work made people laugh.

Ted thought he might be an English teacher. But he didn't always like to study. In class he liked to draw cartoons!

Then he met someone special. Her name was Helen Palmer. Helen thought Ted should draw and write, not teach. Ted knew she was right. They got along so well that soon they were married.

Ted loved to have fun. He was happy when people enjoyed his books and cartoons.

MAKING BOOKS

Ted and Helen lived in New York City. Ted worked for a magazine. Again he drew and wrote cartoons. He started signing his work as "Dr. Seuss."

One cartoon was about Flit bug spray. The Flit company thought the cartoon was very funny. They gave Ted a job making more cartoons.

The Flit cartoons made Ted famous. He was also earning a lot of money. Ted and Helen loved to travel. Now they had enough money to go to faraway lands. They traveled to places like Japan and Africa.

Ted worked in his tower studio, high above the California hills.

Ted liked his work. But he wanted to use more of his **imagination** (i-mah-ji-NAY-shun). Ted had so many great ideas! He thought a children's book was the best way to share them.

It was hard to get his first book published. No one wanted to make *Mulberry Street* into a book. Ted asked 27 companies to publish his book. They all said no. Finally, one publisher said yes.

Children loved this new book by Dr. Seuss. Ted kept on writing and drawing. Soon there were many wonderful Dr. Seuss books. *Horton Hatches the Egg* and *If I Ran the Circus* are two of his early stories.

Ted and Helen moved to **La Jolla** (la HOY-yah), California. They lived in a pink house with a tall pink tower. Ted's **studio** (STOO-dee-oh) was in the tower. This was where he drew, wrote, and thought.

The Cat in the Hat may be Ted's most famous book.

PUZZLING HIS PUZZLER

In 1956 Ted took on a **challenge** (CHA-lenj). Some people thought that beginning reading books were boring. The books did not make it easy for children to learn how to read. Could Dr. Seuss make a book that was both easy and fun?

Ted did make this book. He called it *The Cat in the Hat.* It helped many children learn how to read. They loved the story of this funny cat who came to cheer up two children stuck inside on a rainy day. Children laughed over the giant mess the cat made. *The Cat in the Hat* made Dr. Seuss famous.

In 2004, the Dr. Seuss National Sculpture Garden was opened in Springfield, Massachusetts. Audrey Geisel is standing in front. Behind her is Ted's stepdaughter, Lark Grey Diamond-Cates. She designed and made the garden.

Next, Ted wrote and painted *How the Grinch Stole Christmas!* Once again, his book was a big hit.

In 1957, Ted and Helen Geisel were offered new jobs at Random House Publishers. Ted became the president of the new Beginner Books group. Helen was the vice president. They helped other writers make easy-to-read books, too.

In 1960, Ted took on another challenge. Could he write a book using only 50 words? The head of Random House, a man named Bennett Cerf, made a bet with Ted. He bet Ted $50 that he could not make a book using only 50 words. Ted always loved a good challenge. Back in his office, he started thinking and drawing. Soon he drew Sam-I-Am. He was a friendly little creature with fur. Then he made up a grumpy fellow and a new kind of food. He had it! When *Green Eggs and Ham* was published the cover read, "A 50-Word Book." No other Dr. Seuss book has sold more copies.

Children cook up some green eggs and ham.

Here is proof of how many people read and loved *Green Eggs and Ham.* In 1985, Princeton University honored Dr. Seuss by giving him an award. He was invited to a ceremony to get his award. Instead, he got a big surprise. When his name was called, he walked to the stage. Everyone else stood up. The room was filled with scientists and teachers. Together they repeated: "That Sam-I-Am, That Sam-I-Am, I do not like that Sam-I-Am. I do not like Green Eggs and Ham."

These grown-ups knew the words to *Green Eggs and Ham.* They had read them many years ago, when they first learned how to read. And they all still knew them by heart.

Ted worked very, very hard on each book he wrote. He spent a long time picking the right words. Each color had to be just right, too. Ted called this work "puzzling my puzzler." He believed that children should have the best books he could make.

Audrey Geisel on the Hollywood Walk of Fame, in 2004. She received the star for Ted.

YOUNG AT HEART

Ted turned many of his books into **animated (ah-nah-MAY-ted)** (cartoons that move on the screen) television shows. One of these was *How the Grinch Stole Christmas.* At first Ted was worried. Were the songs good enough? Who would do the Grinch's voice?

But Ted didn't need to worry. In 1966 *The Grinch* was shown for the first time. Right away it was a huge hit. Now it is shown on television every year at Christmas.

Ted liked to read to children. He was glad when kids wrote to him about his books.

Soon after the television *Grinch* was finished, Helen died. A while later Ted married again. His new wife was Audrey Diamond. She and Ted and Helen had been friends for a long time. She also helped him with his writing.

As the years went by, Ted became very famous for his children's books. He sold more and more of them. Though he was very famous, he was still a very private person. He did not like to make public speeches. He did not like to talk with reporters. He did not enjoy talking to adults about his work. He did, though, like to hear from children. Many kids wrote to him and sent him pictures. He saved everything.

Ted won many awards for his books. He won a Peabody award for *How the Grinch Stole Christmas* television special. In 1976, the California Association of Teachers of English gave him its very first Outstanding California Author Award. In 1980, the American Library Association gave him an award for service to

How the Grinch Stole Christmas! became a movie starring Jim Carrey.

children. He even won a Pulitzer Prize. This prize is one of the highest awards given to writers.

Ted kept on drawing and writing for the rest of his life. He was 87 years old when he died on September 24, 1991. On his desk, he left drawings and an unfinished book. His death made headlines the world over. Many people remembered his beloved books.

After his death, his books stayed in print. There were even new books that he was working on when he died. A movie version of *How the Grinch Stole Christmas*, starring Jim Carrey came out in 2000.

Ted always loved fun and was curious about everything. At heart he was still a child. Dr. Seuss will live forever in his books.

Kids all over the world celebrate Dr. Seuss Day in March.

1904	Theodor Seuss Geisel born on March 2 in Springfield, Massachusetts
1925	Graduates from Dartmouth College, New Hampshire
1927	Marries Helen Palmer
1937	Publishes first children's book, *And to Think That I Saw It on Mulberry Street*
1948	Moves to La Jolla, California
1957	First beginning reader book, *The Cat in the Hat*
1966	First television showing of *How the Grinch Stole Christmas!*
1967	Helen dies
1968	Marries Audrey Diamond
1984	Wins Pulitzer Prize
1991	Dies on September 24 in La Jolla, California
2004	To honor his 100th birthday, a Dr. Seuss postage stamp is issued; Dr. Seuss National Memorial Garden opens in Springfield, Massachusetts; the Seussentennial Imagination Tour begins

SELECTED WORKS

1937	*And to Think That I Saw It on Mulberry Street*
1947	*McElligot's Pool*
1950	*If I Ran the Zoo*
1954	*Horton Hears a Who!*
1957	*The Cat in the Hat*
1957	*How the Grinch Stole Christmas!*
1958	*The Cat in the Hat Comes Back*
1960	*One Fish Two Fish Red Fish Blue Fish*
1960	*Green Eggs and Ham*
1963	*Hop on Pop*
1965	*Fox in Socks*
1971	*The Lorax*
1990	*Oh, the Places You'll Go!*

Cohen, Charles. *The Seuss, the Whole Seuss and Nothing But the Seuss: A Visual Biography of Theodor Seuss Geisel.* New York: Random House Books for Young Readers, 2004.

Krull, Kathleen. *The Boy on Fairfield Street.* New York: Random House Books for Young Readers, 2004.

Gaines, Ann Graham. *Dr. Seuss* (A Real-Life Reader Biography). Hockessin, DE: Mitchell Lane Publishers, Inc., 2002.

Rau, Dana Meachen. *Dr. Seuss* (Rookie Biographies). Danbury, CT: Scholastic Library Publishing, 2003.

Weidt, Maryann N. *Oh, the Places He Went: A Story About Dr. Seuss–Theodor Seuss Geisel.* Minneapolis, MN: Carolrhoda Books, 1994.

Paterson, Vincent, dir. *In Search of Dr. Seuss.* Turner Home Video, 1996.

Web Addresses

Biographies of Dr. Seuss online
www.catinthehat.org/

www.seussville.com/morefun/ted.html